She said it with her eyes
He heard it in her smile

by Paula Olmstead

FriesenPress

Suite 300 - 990 Fort St
Victoria, BC, V8V 3K2
Canada

www.friesenpress.com

Copyright © 2016 by Paula Olmstead
First Edition — 2016

All rights reserved.

No part of this publication may be reproduced in any form, or by any means, electronic or mechanical, including photocopying, recording, or any information browsing, storage, or retrieval system, without permission in writing from FriesenPress.

ISBN
978-1-4602-9464-2 (Hardcover)
978-1-4602-9465-9 (Paperback)
978-1-4602-9466-6 (eBook)

1. SELF-HELP

Distributed to the trade by The Ingram Book Company

Table of Contents

Why This Book? 1

Why is it Important? 6

Verbal Communication 13

What is non-verbal communication? 28

Conclusion 57

The Learning Journal 58

This book is dedicated to my family:
Chad (and Jazmine),
Cody (and Tara),
Ashley (and Matthew), Kaden, Tristen
and my husband, Patrick.

Why This Book?

Have you ever been trying to listen to someone else but you've found yourself pretending to listen? Perhaps you are actually thinking about how you are going to respond, or about what you want the other person to be thinking. You might have been thinking about something completely different. But it is possible to learn how to listen more intentionally.

This approach to listening was developed throughout a long period of time. It can become a "listening practice" in the same way that some of you may think of your "yoga practice" or your "mindfulness practice."

Have you ever felt heard on a deeper level by another person? That you have been understood beyond the words you have used?

It is because you've actually been listened to.

Reflective Moment:

Have you ever felt heard on a deeper level? Use the space below to write what it meant to you.

_____

_____

_____

There's no need to worry if you haven't had that happen. Not very many people listen intently or consider the many angles of what is being said. This book is intended to provide you with information to give you insight into how you might have more understanding of what others want you to understand.

Have you ever been trying to listen to someone else but found yourself actually pretending to listen? Perhaps you are thinking about how you are going to respond or what you want the other person to be thinking. You might have been thinking about something completely unrelated such as what you are going to cook for dinner, if your blouse matches your skirt, and so on. You then find yourself having to almost shake your head to concentrate on the conversation. You think to yourself, *Uh-oh. I haven't been paying attention. I wonder what this person is talking about. I'd better listen so I can respond as though I've been listening all along.*

I'm sure we've all had this happen at least once, some maybe have had it happen a half-dozen times, and there are some (you know who you are) who have this happen continually. I've worked with these people as have you.

The situation would go something like this:

"Hi Jane, how's it going?" asks Mary.

"Well, not so good. I had a very difficult weekend. You remember I told you that I had to take my sons to hockey . . . the day began with missing the alarm . . . we had to get to the arena at 6:00 . . . we couldn't find the boys' skates before we left . . . they were in the car . . ." and on it goes until Jane asks, "Have you ever had that happen?"

Mary is now brought back to the conversation by the question. She's been thinking about her weekend, which had actually been quite nice. She went bird watching and saw some new species that she hadn't seen before. They took pictures. She doesn't have children and has no idea what all this hockey talk is about and her mind wandered while Jane was talking. She takes a chance with her response and says, "No, I've never had that happen." It is a safe response because in all likelihood whatever Jane is talking about hasn't happened to her.

Now that you've read an actual example of what I am describing, is it starting to make sense that sometimes we are not listening as closely as we could be?

Reflective Moment:

Has this happened to you? Who were you talking with?

_____

_____

_____

_____

What might you have missed that the person was saying?

_____

_____

_____

_____

What did you start thinking about instead of listening?

_____

_____

_____

_____

_____

Did the person you were speaking with realize that you were not listening to what he or she was saying?

_____

_____

_____

_____

_____

If you have no idea what I'm talking about, then this book is likely for you, and you might consider being open to the need for it.

Reread this section to see if you were actually paying attention to what you were reading. I know that sometimes it is just as hard to take in what one is reading as it is to hear what people are saying.

If you do know what I am talking about when I describe this application of listening, this book is for you as well, because you will be able to develop your practice of listening. Everyone can further their skills in this area. Some of you, perhaps, already have the talent I am describing and this will simply be a refresher for you.

Reflective Moment:

Is this a refresher for you or is this new for you? Why?

_____

_____

_____

_____

_____

I hope this book is helpful for you and I hope by sharing this gift, I am making communication in this world a little better. The world needs some help in the communication area and effective listening beyond the words may be just what it needs.

Why is it Important?

This book is important because it is about an aspect of listening that is so very, very critical and for which there are limited practical, genuine books to guide people on how to listen beyond the words. There are definitions and there is theory, but there just isn't as much practical advice as would be beneficial to all of us.

So much in life revolves around communication. Effective communication only occurs when effective listening has occurred. If you don't know what I mean, then you might very well be missing out on what is so important about effectively communicating with others.

To get the most from this book, you will need to actually apply the thoughts that you find helpful to your communication. Ideally, you will read a bit, ponder what you have read, and reflect on how you may or may not be applying each particular component of effective listening. I have attempted to make it easy for you and to give you time to think by actually including space with a graphic reminding you to "ponder" what you have read. I have prompted your thinking by adding a question. Or, for those of you who just like to get through something to be able to say you've done it, read the book cover to cover. But even if you read through the book from front to back, I hope you will go back through it again, think about the concepts, and write your thoughts.

She said it with her eyes He heard it in her smile

Either way, you'll get the most from this book if you think about how you currently apply the concepts and consider how you might apply them in the future to develop your listening. This book is not intended to be critical of how you listen. We can all be better at listening—myself included. It requires practice. In fact, it would benefit everyone to grow in this practice of listening. Contrary to the saying that practice makes perfect...practice makes us better.

No one is perfect, particularly in the area of communication and listening. There are so many nuances at play that we cannot possibly get it completely right, but we can certainly become better and better. If we learn to listen well beyond just the words being spoken, others will feel heard. Imagine a world where everyone feels heard. This would be a fabulous goal for everyone. In the meantime, if just one or two people are reached through this book, listening will have improved in our world.

Definitions

In order to understand this book and to follow the thinking, it would be valuable to have a shared understanding of the words "listen" and "hear," and of the difference between non-verbal communication and verbal communication.

The *Oxford* dictionary defines listen as "give one's attention to a sound; take notice of and act on what someone says; respond to advice or a request."[1] The *Cambridge* dictionary online distinguishes between the words hear and listen and tells us that "hearing is an event; it is something which happens to us as a natural process, while listening is an action; it is something we do consciously."[2]

---

1   www.oxforddictionaries.com/definition/english/listen (accessed January 30, 2016).

2   http://dictionary.cambridge.org/grammar/british-grammar/hear-or-listen-to (accessed January 30, 2016).

This is an extremely important concept that you may not have spent much time thinking about. For example, let's think about this sentence about hearing: *I heard it rain last night.* It happened. I heard it. It is over.

Now, think about these sentences about listening: *I was listening to my son this morning. He said he was looking forward to his dad opening his Father's Day gift.* I could see the excitement in his face. He was beaming. I could tell that he believed he had understood what was important to his dad, and he had purchased something that was perfect. Both he and I were consciously thinking about what he was saying.

As it turned out, the gift was indeed perfect.

So, take a moment to ponder.

Reflective Moment:

What have you been hearing?

_____

_____

_____

_____

_____

How have you been listening?

_____

_____

It is also important for us to have a shared understanding of non-verbal communication. Wikipedia tells us that "nonverbal communication between people is communication through sending and receiving wordless [mostly visual] cues"[3] between people.

So, take a moment to ponder.

Reflective Moment:

What nonverbal communication have you or others around you been using?

And finally, verbal communication is defined as "use of sounds and words to express yourself, especially in contrast to using gestures or mannerisms (non-verbal communications)."[4] According to

---

3   https://en.wikipedia.org/wiki/Nonverbal_Communication (accessed January 30, 2016).

4   http://www.yourdictionary.com/verbal-communications (accessed January 30, 2016).

the Global Language Monitor the number of words in the English language is 1,035,877.3.[5] It seems likely we don't all use more than a million words. We probably have our favorites.

So, take a moment to ponder.

Reflective Moment:

What words are your favorites?

_____

_____

_____

_____

Reflect a few more moments:

Are there words you use that allow everyone to understand what you mean?

_____

_____

_____

_____

_____

---

5   http://www.languagemonitor.com/number-of-words/no-of-words (accessed January 30, 2016).

She said it with her eyes He heard it in her smile

Are they current sayings that everyone uses?

_____

_____

_____

_____

_____

Do only you and your friends understand the words?

_____

_____

_____

_____

If some of the words that are used are current slang they can have completely different meanings to people who don't use them. Perhaps an example here will make this easier to understand. Currently the word "sick" is used by some to mean "cool," while those of us who might use the word "cool," think the word "sick" is used to describe someone who is not feeling well. Describing a song or a pet as sick to some people might mean these things are cool; to others the use of the word sick means they are not doing well; they are unhealthy or unwell.

If you didn't have words to add on the lines for your favorites and/or you automatically answered that of course everyone understands what you mean, and you found yourself nodding your head—I can imagine some of you doing that—go back and re-ponder; it might be quite enlightening for you.

Hmm . . .

Okay, so far we've taken a very, very high level look (the fifty-thousand-foot version) at hearing and listening, and verbal and non-verbal. If any of these concepts are confusing or you are unclear on how I am distinguishing between them, feel free to go back and reread the first section of this book. The remainder of the book assumes you are following along with me.

If I were looking at you and actually saying these words to you, and your non-verbal cues, such as a particular expression on your face, suggested that you were confused, puzzled, not following along, or had skipped a bit by reading very quickly—no worries. Those non-verbal cues showed that we are not on the same page. Please go back and re-read this first section.

Now, with the basic definitions and understanding of these concepts understood and under your belt, let's move along and do a deep dive into the most important topics.

Verbal Communication

Verbal communication is generally the easiest of the concepts. People talk and we listen. Remember, listening is an action that we do consciously. We are focused on the person who is talking and we are paying attention to the words, the sentences, and the content of what is being said. Let's assume you are following along with what the person is saying.

Let's look at a few examples to ensure we understand this concept in the same way.

> Example 1: "I am going to the fruit stand to buy some peaches."

You have listened, and you know that the speaker is buying some peaches (not just any fruit but peaches) at the fruit stand (not just anywhere). The person (not we) is going to buy (and not barter for) the peaches. Perhaps you have not often thought this hard about a sentence. You are also seeing how easy it is for an eleven-word sentence to be easily misinterpreted without the speaker intending for that to happen. Just take one of the alternatives (the phrases in parentheses) and the meaning of the sentence changes substantially. Here are the alternatives based on the possible misinterpretation that could happen if someone were not listening closely:

"We are going to the fruit stand to buy some peaches." Who is we and why is someone else going with you? Are you picking them up? Are they coming here?

"I am going to the fruit stand to buy some bananas." We already have some—why are you buying those?

"I am going to the fruit stand to buy some fruit." What kind? Why? We don't like fruit.

"I am going to the store to buy some fruit." Why would you go to the store and not the fruit stand?

"I am going to the community store [the speaker refuses to shop at regular stores or fruit markets] and I am going to exchange [the speaker always barters rather than uses money] some of my hand-made soap [he doesn't have much money and pays everyone with his soap] for some peaches."

You might think a person isn't listening very closely to come up with this alternative, but if you are open to what is in the brackets as you are reading this, then it makes sense that it might happen. It also could easily happen if the listener were thinking about his or her past history with the speaker and wasn't very focused on what the speaker was currently saying.

Reflective Moment:

Insert a sentence of your own choosing:

_____

_____

_____

_____

_____

She said it with her eyes He heard it in her smile   **15**

Write a few variations of what might be interpreted to be
the meaning:

_____

_____

_____

_____

_____

Listen to all the conversations around you and see how long it takes
you to come across a conversation in which the receiver of the
information clearly did not understand the message of the speaker.
How long did it take?

_____

_____

What was the conversation?

_____

_____

_____

_____

_____

Volume of Speech

Another interesting area worth exploring within verbal communication is how loudly people speak. This is quite dependent on the individual. Some individuals speak loudly because they are hearing impaired. If that is the case, none of the following should be considered.

However, if they are not hearing impaired, here are a few items for your consideration. People generally fall into one of three categories: loud speakers, quiet speakers, and those who speak at an average volume. The average volume of speech is simply a normal level of speech. There isn't anything particular to consider in that case.

If the person speaks loudly or quietly it is worthwhile considering. Typically, people who speak overly loudly seem to feel they have to yell in order to command the attention of others.

Reflective Moment:

Do you know someone or more than one person who speaks very, very loudly? What causes him or her to do this? The answer to this question tells you something about the person that will be helpful for you to know when you are communicating with him or her.

_____

_____

_____

If someone speaks quietly, there are two general explanations for this. One is that the person is very shy and doesn't want to be seen as intrusive. The other explanation is that the person is actually very confident with himself or herself and with his or her communication style. People who are shy see no need to be at the average volume level, which is often louder than they would comfortably be speaking. They certainly see no need to be loud and yell.

Reflective Moment:

Do you know people who speak very quietly? Do you spend the time to hear what they are saying so that you can benefit from it?

_____

_____

_____

_____

Once you have the speaker's general volume of speech figured out, you will want to pay attention to when it changes. Typically, if a loud speaker is speaking quietly or a quiet speaker is speaking loudly, this is a signal that you need to pay careful attention to what he (or she) is saying. The change in volume likely means that these people are feeling stress or pressure, and what they are saying is important to understand.

Reading Between the Lines of Verbal Conversation

From here on, things are going to get very interesting. We have covered the topics of hearing and listening, and verbal and non-verbal communication at a very high level. We then explored in more detail verbal communication and the fact that unless we are truly listening very deeply we may quickly misunderstand the speaker's words and the intention behind the words. We are now going to explore and ponder what is between the lines in verbal communication.

Reflective Moment:

Write down what you think reading between the lines of verbal conversation means.

_____

_____

_____

_____

According to YourDictionary.com, reading between the lines means to "infer a meaning that is not stated explicitly."[6] This means that you listen to what is being said, you hear the words, and then you consider what is actually meant by the words.

For example, sarcasm requires one to read between the lines because what is being said is often what is not meant. On a very, very hot day you meet your friend for coffee. Sweat is pouring down her forehead and she is clearly not comfortable. She says, "I just

---

6   read-between-the-lines (n.d.) Retrieved August 3, 2015 from http://www.yourdictionary.com/read-between-the-lines.

love the heat!" Now, on the surface this would sound like she is enjoying the high temperature. However, you know she is uncomfortable and you guess that what she really means is, "This is too hot." You ask if she'd like to sit in the shade rather than soak up the heat at the table directly in the sun. She replies that, yes, she'd like to do that.

You enjoy the heat and can't imagine that she wouldn't enjoy it as well. If you hadn't read between the lines, you would have thought that she liked the heat and you would have happily sat at the table in the sun.

This example is pretty straightforward once you learn to pick up when someone is using sarcasm. There is often a tone in the voice that suggests the person doesn't really believe what he or she is saying, or the facial expression, usually a grin, doesn't align with the words being said. There are many examples of the use of sarcasm. Listen closely when someone makes any of the following statements: "This is great weather." "What a wonderful location." "What a nice color for a car." "Look at the happy couple." "What a wonderful child; wouldn't you like to have one or two?" You can quickly understand that the context in which these statements are being spoken may alter the meaning of what is being said. You may have to ask probing questions to confirm that the person is actually being sarcastic.

What is not so easy to do is to hear the actual words being said and to consider their real meaning. Sometimes, what is being said is exactly what someone is meaning to say and meaning for you to hear. Other times, there is an entire series of words that is being thought, but is not being said out loud.

For example: "The sky is blue. There are a few clouds. It is a nice day."

This seems very straightforward, but what if these words were being said while there was a pile of very dark, menacing clouds in the west, and storms come from the west where you live? What if you could hear thunder off in the distance? What if you could see lightning in the clouds? What if the weather forecast that morning was for serious weather with warnings and watches likely for the area in which you live? This context is not in alignment with the words that are in quotation marks above. What is between the words that are quoted above? Perhaps this is an optimistic person who is hoping for the best and is only saying positive words. Perhaps the person is actually saying, "The sky is blue right now, but I don't think it is going to stay that way for long. There are a few clouds, but just look at those clouds that are on their way here. It is a nice day right now, but we'd better get indoors quickly or we are going to get caught in a horrible rainstorm, thunderstorm, or worse—a tornado."

Here's an example that you might have heard said by a family member or by someone in a work setting. Your colleague or family member is looking out of sorts—a bit sad or discouraged. Her eyebrows are furrowed as though she is thinking deeply. It appears that her eyes may be filling with tears.

"Is everything okay?" you ask.

"It's fine, just fine," she replies, and looks away from you.

You could take this response at face value for the words as they are said, but do you really think everything is okay with her? If you probe this family member or colleague, you will likely hear that there is a problem. The response, if you follow up, will likely be something like, "It's fine except for the terrible fight I just had with my brother, and I don't think we will ever get along." This may now lead to a conversation about what is really going on for the person and how she is really feeling. If it is a family situation, the individual may be able to seek out assistance in how to address this problem. If it is at work that an employee responds with this information, it may be that she would benefit from a conversation with a counselor. If the issue is addressed properly, she may be able to become significantly more productive at work, as her focus is not getting distracted by the troubling family situation. As you can see, the initial words said are sometimes not what is actually meant, and if left unexplored may lead to difficulties for the individual and ultimately, perhaps, for you as well.

Here's another example of the same phrase. Years ago, at one of the large businesses in which I worked, some employees were extremely dissatisfied with the way they were being treated by their supervisor. The supervisor was treating them as dispensable and replaceable. It was a patronizing and demeaning place to work. As the days, weeks, and then months of this behavior continued, employees went to senior management to have the issue resolved. Although they were told it would be "fixed," employees didn't see any change in their supervisor's behavior. So, they started very quietly reaching out to a third party—the union—to see if the union would consider helping. Employees became less vocal in the workplace as they reached out to this sophisticated external assistance.

Management started noticing the sudden increasingly quiet behavior of employees. When asked how things were going, the employees would respond, "Just fine." The union had told the employees to use this phrase, "just fine," because it would prevent management from asking more questions. Management started believing that everything was indeed okay. However, it was far from okay. It only seemed okay because the employees had convinced the third party to seriously consider helping them. Cards were signed and the labor board approved the application from the union. Had the management team thought to consider that the words did not match the feeling in the room during team meetings or when they saw employees in the hallways talking in small groups, or if they had asked employees more about how things were going, they might not have had the complexity of a third party introduced into their employment relationship with these employees.

I spoke with the union about what had been the turning point at which employees signed the cards. As you can imagine, it was when the employees had tested the use of the phrase, "just fine." To their disappointment, the management team took the words at face value and didn't follow up. I still have a bit of an emotional reaction of sadness and a sick feeling in the pit of my stomach when I hear employees say, "just fine."

I have worked with many unions over the years and have chatted with several of them about this specific unionizing drive. We agreed that it is sad that employers would choose to take the words at face value, even though other behaviors suggested that the employees were not actually fine. I don't know if unions are still encouraging employees to use this phrase in the manner I've described, but if so, this would suggest that many employers are still not listening to what employees are saying in any deeper sense than just the words.

I have also shared this situation with several employers who were noticing a change in the behavior of their non-unionized employees. Most of these management members were concerned that their employees might not have been being completely forthright about how they were actually feeling.

Reflective Moment:

What do you think about your ability to read between the lines?

Reflective Moment:

 What "aha" thoughts (meaning, wow, I haven't thought of that before) are you having?

_____

_____

_____

_____

_____

Let's consider a couple more examples of reading between the lines, which are work-related but could just as easily be between family members or friends. We'll review three examples, each of which will become more complex.

Our first example is you and a colleague working on a task together. This work is something that you do on an ongoing basis, while your colleague is new to it. As you and the colleague are working, your colleague is decreasing the speed at which the work is being accomplished. So, you ask your colleague if the task is understood.

"Yes, of course," he says. "You explained it to me and I think I understand it."

You could take this as the response and simply continue on with the work. However, if you looked closely at your colleague's face you'd see that he is not smiling and actually appears to be concentrating very hard on the task. Or you could pick up on a couple of the phrases and words in his reply to you. The term "of course" could be used to imply that it would be silly to think he might answer you with "maybe" or "no." Further, notice that the term

"I think" is used in the second sentence. This could mean he does understand it. Or it could actually mean, "I'm not sure, but I think I understand." This is quite different than choosing the word "know." The sentence, "You explained it to me and I think I understand it," is very different than, "You explained it to me and I know I understand it." Do you see the difference? Only one word is changed in the sentence but the meaning of this response is very different. If you missed the word "think" and were thinking the person said, "know," you would completely miss what the person is communicating to you. This may seem complex, but it is really quite simple. It means we need to listen to every word that someone says to us.

Reflective Moment:

Pay attention to the way you are listening to others. Do you think you have heard all the words the person is saying?

_____

_____

_____

_____

Here's another example of reading between the lines. Have you ever been in a discussion that is highly emotional, with the participants having several very passionate perspectives or approaches on something? In all likelihood, this conflict has been going on for some time, either in that meeting or during a series of meetings, and the participants are getting frustrated with each other.

At some point, one person is going to state that, "This isn't getting us very far and isn't helpful to anyone." This person then suggests the participants should agree on one approach to use. He or she will likely even say that everyone's ideas are very good and that each of the ideas has some great points. If you haven't experienced this, you won't know what happens next. Pay attention and learn, though, because it is all about reading between the lines.

In most cases, what the person is actually saying is: "You all have some good ideas, but we need to agree on one and we are going to try my idea." Those clearly aren't the words that were said, but that meaning is what is between the words. The next sentence that will likely be said is, "I'd suggest we try one of the approaches. Let's test out mine." Typically, as the other participants weren't expecting this to happen next, and given that they have already agreed with the previous statements, they feel compelled to agree. If only they had been reading between the lines of what was said and anticipating where the person was going with his or her sentences, they may have asked some questions or made some argument to consider *all* the options presented by the participants.

Reflective Moment:

What aha thoughts are you having?

_____

_____

_____

_____

Here is one more example of reading between the lines in a difficult situation. It could be a discussion between family members; a negotiation in a team of students assigned to do a case study together; or a work situation, in which a team is exploring options. Several ideas have been put on the table for consideration. Then, one of the participants states that the pros and cons of each of the suggestions should be discussed. The looks on the other participants' faces are skeptical. But everyone says that it's okay to discuss it. A great deal of time is then spent on reviewing the pros and cons of each of the ideas. What is not being stated by any of the participants is that actually, of the five suggestions, three don't make sense financially or from some other perspective. If someone had read between the lines of what the participants were saying and combined that with the skeptical look on everyone's faces, a great deal of time could have been saved. If that same someone had stated something like, "I don't think three of these options are feasible for us," and then explained the rationale, the time would likely have been better spent on the two more workable options. This is a bit complicated, so read through this example again.

It is very difficult to see or hear what is happening in a situation like this if you are actually directly involved in it, unless you have considered what I describe above. It is very easy to get caught up in what is being suggested, as it seems as though the team is making progress and is using its time effectively. However, if one chooses to read between the lines of what is being said by each of the individuals and the skeptical look of each, a few probing questions on the feasibility of the options will go a long way.

Reflective Moment:

What do you think you are doing well to read between the lines?

_____

_____

_____

Reflective Moment:

What could you do better to give yourself more opportunity to read between the lines?

_____

_____

_____

What is non-verbal communication?

As described in footnote three, non-verbal communication is the process of sending and receiving wordless (mostly visual) cues between people. Sometimes, non-verbal communication is as important, if not maybe more important, than verbal communication. This is possibly because people have been trained to be careful about what they say. They hold back in a conversation rather than having a direct and important communication with another person. What they do, however, is demonstrate various non-verbal signals that, when acknowledged, usually tell the actual story.

I hope I haven't lost you here, but please have patience. It will all make so much sense as you think this through.

Types of non-verbal communication include movements of the eyes or the mouth; the head in various positions; facial expressions; body language, (including a person's posture and changes to the posture); movements of the hands and their positions; and the proximity of the speaker to you and others in the conversation as well as the significant use or unplanned application of silence.

I'll go through each of these in some detail, so bear with me as I describe them. There may be much to learn. As you've discovered up to this point in this book, I will include some lines for you to capture your thoughts as you are reading through each of these components of non-verbal communication.

At this point, we've covered definitions of verbal and non-verbal communication as well as reading between the lines of verbal communication.

Reflective Moment:

What have you learned about your communication thus far?

_____

_____

_____

_____

Reflective Moment:

What aha thoughts have you had while reading this part of the book?

_____

_____

_____

_____

What is non-verbal communication?

Non-verbal communication is the way that living beings communicate without actually speaking.

Have you been around dogs? Your own? Your friend's? When a dog wants your attention, it will come up to you and look at you. If you've had an expressive dog that you've taken the time to get to know, the non-verbal communication of the love in their eyes and posture can be distinguished between: I need to go out, I want you to scratch my ears, or let's play. If you have had such a dog you know what I am describing. If you haven't owned or known an expressive dog, ask a dog owner about this. Most dog owners will be more than happy to talk to you about their "Fido" and how Fido makes it perfectly clear what it wants without being able to speak.

People communicate non-verbally as well in a variety of ways, including using their eyes, their mouths, the positioning of the head, their facial expressions, movements of the body and hands, their posture, their proximity to others, touching, and silence.

Non-verbal communication is an extremely important form of communication. So much is missed or misunderstood because people don't pay attention to these aspects of communication.

Reflective Moment:

Do you pay attention to non-verbal communication?

_____

_____

_____

_____

She said it with her eyes He heard it in her smile

Or do you just listen to the words or not look at the person?

Reflective Moment:

What have you learned about your communication thus far?

_____

_____

_____

_____

What percentage of the time do you actually look at and truly pay attention to non-verbal cues?

_____

_____

_____

What prevents you from paying attention to non-verbal cues?

_____

_____

_____

EYES

Let's begin with the eyes. It is said that the eyes are the windows to the soul. If you haven't been paying attention to non-verbal communication, you may not even understand this concept.

Reflective Moment:

What percent of the time do you look people in the eye?

_____

When you see someone on the street?

_____

When you are talking to someone?

_____

When someone is talking to you?

_____

When a homeless person is speaking to you?

_____

One way to begin to understand this is to start looking people in the eye when you look at them and certainly when you speak to them. If you've already been doing this, increase the percentage of time until you can get to 100 percent.

	Now	Target #1	Target #2
Look people in the eye	_____	_____	_____
See someone on the street	_____	_____	_____
When you are talking with someone	_____	_____	_____
When someone is talking with you	_____	_____	_____

Revisit this page and revise your target. You will be surprised about how this is going to increase your communication with others.

There are several reasons for this increased communication. First and most simply, people will think you are more interested in them as people. You may, in fact, learn more about the others you come into contact with.

Then, if you take an even deeper dive into this concept, you are going to notice some interesting things about eyes. Eyes can be extremely expressive and can communicative without words. Eyes, combined with eyebrows, may reveal any of the following: sadness, happiness, confusion, surprise, interest, anger, frustration, being closed off, or being inviting and open. The following illustrations help to explain this concept.

I trust now that I have you focused on this, it is making a great deal of sense. I expect you agree that the eyes talk a great deal and communicate a lot without verbal communication. Perhaps you have noticed additional expressions in those around you. Feel free to add a word and draw a picture to remind of you of what it looks like.

She said it with her eyes He heard it in her smile

Space for your hand-drawn picture

(insert word)

Space for your hand-drawn picture

(insert word)

Space for your hand-drawn picture

(insert word)

Space for your hand-drawn picture

(insert word)

This is what makes eyes expressive. They are telling you, or communicating if you will, something about the person you are looking at and how that person may be feeling.

Now that you are either starting to look people in the eye or increasing how often you do it, if you were doing it already, I caution you about the following: There's a fine line between looking at a person's eyes and staring at them. You will want to keep the look to a short, three-second count: 1—1000, 2—1000, 3—1000. Much longer and it feels to the person you are looking at that you are rudely staring at them. You'll know you have over-extended the look if they get bashful and look away or if they ask you, "What are you looking at?" which may be accompanied by an angry tone.

Another aspect of eyes is whether they are moving or not. If they are not moving it is so much easier to look into someone's eyes. However, if they are moving and the person is not looking you in the eye, this is another form of communication. Often, if people are not being truthful, they will not look you in the eye. They may just look away. If their eyes are moving back and forth from left to right, that may be communicating that they are shy or uncomfortable with looking at you. It may be that they are self-conscious. It may also be that they are not being truthful with you. There is an entire field of psychology that has studied eye movements and determined that there is meaning if the person looks left or right, and that in general, if the person looks up, that person may be lying. While I have been trained in this way of analyzing eyes (and you may wish to pursue that separately from this book), I prefer to keep it simple. If the person is prepared to look you in the eye, this is a good thing. If the person is not willing to look you in the eye, that's when it's time to get curious about the behavior and why it is happening.

Another interesting aspect of the eyes is who the person looks at when he or she is speaking or non-verbally communicating. If you are not the only one conversing with a person, you may want to watch who else this person looks at or doesn't look at when he or she is speaking. Does the person look at everyone by panning all across the audience that is speaking with him or her? This shows that he or she wants to engage everyone in what he or she is saying.

The person may stop panning to spend a few minutes extra looking at one person, two people, or more people within the group with whom he or she is speaking. This typically means that these speakers want to ensure that they have the attention of those people. There can be many reasons for this and they include: They have already discussed the topic and they are looking for others to join them in the discussion. They are uncomfortable with what they are discussing, and they are looking to the colleagues that tend to support them for some encouragement and reassurance. They are looking directly at the people they think will not support what they are saying, to see how those individuals are reacting. They may be nervous, and are focusing on one or two people because they are scared to look directly at all the others.

As you can see, there can be many explanations for this behavior but these ideas are worth considering as you listen more intently, with a focus on the eyes.

If the person is speaking to a group and doesn't appear to be looking directly at anyone or even panning across the audience, this typically means they are just very nervous, that they don't actually believe what they are saying, or that they are not telling the truth or being honest with their communication. To avoid this interpretation, many public speaking organizations will tell speakers to look at the tops of the heads of the audience. This will give the impression that they are actually engaged with the audience. If you think a speaker might be doing this, rub the top of your head when you see him or her look your way and you'll see the speaker shudder a bit and look confused. This person was not actually looking at the individuals in the audience and was avoiding eye contact. Again, this might mean something and could be considered in relation to the thoughts on individual eye contact mentioned above.

As you can see, how a person looks at the person or the group of people he or she is speaking to, is communicating something. You will need to assess what messages you are getting by considering the person the individual looks at and why you think that is the case—whether this speaker doesn't look directly at anyone or just appears extremely nervous while communicating.

The eyes are among the most powerful non-verbal communication tools. This is actually why they are mentioned in this book's title. I am a generally quiet person and it was through my eyes—which happen to be large and expressive—that my husband "saw" a look of enthusiasm and curiosity when we first met.

So much is said with the eyes.

Mouth

We are also able to "say" a great deal with our mouths without actually having words come from them. We do that by the positioning of our mouths and whether they are open or closed. Most people haven't paid much attention to this area of non-verbal communication, but if you do start paying attention, you will "hear" more than you have to this point.

A smile communicates encouragement and enthusiasm.

An open smile encourages openness and positivity.

A grin can communicate superiority or if the grin is shared, it communicates a connection or shared understanding.

Pouty lips communicate someone not getting their way.

Lips with teeth showing and biting the lower lip show anger.

I suspect these graphics demonstrate to you just how well the lips can communicate a message. Let's think about some lip positions that you have seen and what they mean to you. Add in a word to describe the lips and then draw the lips in the space for the picture to remind you of what is being communicated by those lips.

Space for your hand-drawn picture

(insert word)

Space for your hand-drawn picture

(insert word)

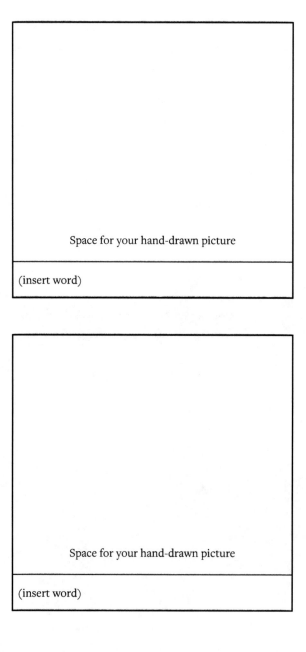

As noted in the title of this book, a smile can communicate a great deal to the observer of the positioning of the mouth.

Reflective Moment:

What do you think is meant by the phrase, "He heard it in her smile"?

_____

_____

_____

In my particular application of this saying, in the context of the title, it meant an encouraging, "yes."

If you want to take this analysis to the next level, consider what the combination of a look in the eyes and an expression at the lips means. What is being communicated?

I think this combination says "hello" or "welcome" and is inviting conversation, either through a similar response from the individual it is being sent to or through verbal communication.

Take some time today and watch the eyes and lip combinations that those around you use. Feel free to record them here and add a word to describe what they mean. What do you "hear" from these eye and mouth combinations?

Space for your hand-drawn picture

(insert word)

Space for your hand-drawn picture

(insert word)

She said it with her eyes He heard it in her smile

```
┌─────────────────────────────┐
│                             │
│                             │
│                             │
│                             │
│                             │
│                             │
│   Space for your hand-drawn │
│            picture          │
├─────────────────────────────┤
│ (insert word)               │
└─────────────────────────────┘
```

Reflective Moment:

What are you learning?

_____

_____

_____

_____

Positions of the Head

There are many different positions possible for the head; however, the two most common are simply looking forward or a sideways tilt. Typically, people holding their heads straight and looking forward are listening or looking at whoever is speaking to them. If the head is tilted sideways, it often means that the individual is making the choice to think deeply about what is being communicated or is confused about what message the communicator is sending.

Facial Expressions

Facial expressions are very communicative with or without words to accompany them. The most common facial expressions that combine eyes, mouth, and position of the head are happy, sad, surprised, confused, or elated. We have all seen the facial expression that demonstrates anger. It is important to pay attention to facial expressions because sometimes the words people use and what they are saying do not actually communicate what they are thinking. The facial expressions that you can see are often telling the individual's true feelings about what is going on. The words that are being used may align with the facial expression, but more often than not polite words are masking how the person actually feels about something. It is good to watch for the alignment of the facial expressions with the words because if they align it confirms that you have understood how the person is feeling. Most often there is alignment with happiness, elation, and sadness.

Pay particular attention when the facial expression denotes anger, frustration, or surprise. People will often mask what they are actually thinking. The understanding of facial expressions can usually benefit by probing the individual for a deeper exploration of what is going on. The most common example of not communicating with words is anger. Have a look at the graphic below and the words that accompany it. Do you really think everything is okay?

"Everything is fine. Just fine."   "No need for concern. I'm fine."

Both of these individuals would benefit from a follow-up probing question: "Your facial expression looks like you might be angry. Would you please explain that to me?" It is critical not to ask a question such as "Is that correct?" or "Would you explain that?" as the respondent will likely answer with the word "no" and you have lost your opportunity to understand what is really going on.

Watch people when you are speaking with them or when two people are talking with each other. It takes some detailed observation, so don't despair if you don't see it right away. You will come across examples, as they happen on a regular basis.

Describe the words that were said.
Draw a picture of what the person's facial expression looked like.

Describe the words that were said.
Draw a picture of what the person's facial expression looked like.

She said it with her eyes He heard it in her smile

Describe the words that were said.
Draw a picture of what the person's facial expression looked like.

Describe the words that were said.
Draw a picture of what the person's facial expression looked like.

I hope you were able to find some examples. Being able to identify facial expression and words that conflict with each other is a very, very important skill. Many people don't take the time to pay attention, but you will be doing this. The more you do it, the more people will appreciate how intently you are listening to them.

Reflective Moment:

What have you learned about your communication thus far?

_____

_____

_____

_____

Hands

Have you noticed that some people speak with their hands? You'll see them use their hands as they are talking. People who use their hands while talking aren't just flailing them around. Hands are used to emphasize their message. If they want to encourage openness and conversation they will often emphasize their message by opening their hands.

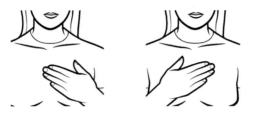

Or speakers will place their hands above their hearts to emphasize how emotionally connected they are to whatever they are talking about.

Or speakers will place their hands in the middle of their chests to emphasize that they are speaking about a personal perspective they have about something; usually this action corresponds with the word "I."

Reflective Moment:

Watch those around you to see how often they use their hands. What action are they doing and what does it mean to them?

_____

_____

_____

_____

Posture

People stand in a variety of ways. Some people stand very straight. Other people don't stand straight but with a slight slouch. Others stand with their weight leaning to one side or the other.

How people stand is not what is important as regards communication. It is the changes in posture that speak volumes without the person saying a word. If a person usually stands very straight with his or her shoulders back but has changed his or her posture to slouching or leaning, this usually means a change. The person may have changed from being very confident in what he or she is saying to being unsure. Alternatively, the person may have realized that the way he or she was standing was intimidating to the person being addressed and thus changed his or her posture to be softer and more open.

Reflective Moment:

Over the next few days, watch the posture of people who speak with you. How are they standing? What do you think it means? Did their posture change during the conversation? Why?

_____

_____

_____

_____

Proximity to others

Another non-verbal but very communicative behavior is how close someone stands to the person with whom he or she is communicating. As you've likely heard, we all have a personal space that we are comfortable with. One inch into the personal space and we become uncomfortable. The more the speaker moves into another person's personal space, the more uncomfortable that person becomes and the less that person is hearing. A caring person will notice the other person's discomfort and will move out of his or her personal space.

Reflective Moment:

Keeping this in mind, have you experienced people speaking with you who stand more closely than you are comfortable with?

_____

_____

_____

_____

Reflective Moment:

Have you experienced people speaking with you who stand farther away from you than you think they should, giving you the impression that they are uncomfortable with you?

_____

_____

_____

_____

Now that you've thought about the proximity of people who speak to you, let's make it personal. Where you stand makes a difference to the people you are communicating with.

Reflective Moment:

How close do you stand to other people when you are speaking to them? Do you think you might have made others uncomfortable by either being too close or too far away?

_____

_____

_____

_____

Silence

The last area that I encourage you to explore is silence. Even though silence is not verbally saying something or using any of the other non-verbal aspects we have explored, it often communicates a great deal.

We sometimes think of silence as a person ignoring us. It is usually the exact opposite. In reality, people might not know what to say and are using silence for a moment to compose their thoughts before they speak. Or they know exactly what they want to say, but they are holding back in speaking. If you aren't paying very close attention, you are going to miss this. You will find that people have patterns with their use of silence. Figure out who uses it and why they are using it. The best way to understand why people use silence is to ask them to explain it to you. Why are they silent? What are they thinking? You will be surprised how much you will learn from silence.

Reflective Moment:

How do those around you use silence?

_____

_____

_____

_____

Communication through touch

Another way to communicate is through touch. This is not "sexual" touch but simply placement of a hand on an arm or a shoulder. Now, there are people who do not like to have their personal space intruded upon and who certainly do not like to have someone place his or her hand on them. However, for people who are comfortable with touch, there is a great deal that can be communicated without words through touch.

In the most innocent of applications, this is an example: When you see someone you know in sorrow with tears, you want to comfort him or her. The person may tell you about a sorrowful situation, which is causing great grief. A simple touch on the shoulder acknowledges, without words, that you care.

Reflective Moment:

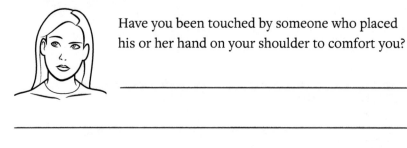

Have you been touched by someone who placed his or her hand on your shoulder to comfort you?

_____

_____

_____

Reflective Moment:

Did it cause you comfort?

_____

_____

_____

_____

Conclusion

I have enjoyed sharing the techniques I use to "hear" people beyond the words. It is my gift to you, if you will. I hope you will benefit from these techniques. Paying attention to the meaning between the words being said, what is not being said, and all the non-verbal cues including the movements of the eyes and the mouth, the head position, the facial expressions, the gestures of the hands, as well as silence, and touch will enable you to hear even more than you do now.

I have been thinking about sharing this gift with you for more than a year, and I hope to have described it in an enabling way. I want others to understand how to employ the book's techniques and wish for you to see the value in applying these ideas.

I continue to develop this talent in myself and others and expect there will be a follow-up to this book, which will describe the concept further. Until then, re-read this book, use the Reflective Moments again and again, and I expect others around you will "hear" and feel that you have increased your ability to really hear them and communicate effectively.

Warm regards to you and all those with whom you communicate,
Paula Olmstead

The Learning Journal

This section is for those of you who would like a way to do more reflection or practice. Listening effectively requires practice. You may want to practice all the techniques described in this book, or you may want to only practice some of them. Each individual has his or her own preference for how to reflect upon and practice listening skills.

With that in mind, I have provided thirty-one pages for Reflection and Practice.

The topics of listening that I have shared with you fall into three categories:

1. Volume of Speech,
2. Reading Between the Lines
3. Non-verbal. Non-verbal includes:
    - eyes
    - mouth
    - head
    - facial expressions
    - the hands and their positions
    - posture
    - changes to posture
    - proximity
    - silence
    - touch

Pick a topic, make a goal for the topic and give it a try.

I hope you experience happiness through your reflection and practice of these skills.

Day 1—Topic 1

_____

Your goal for the topic:

_____

_____

_____

_____

What did you observe about yourself or others?

_____

_____

_____

_____

Capture your reflections on what you observed. What did you learn?

_____

_____

_____

_____

Day 2—Topic 2

Your goal for the topic:

What did you observe about yourself or others?

Capture your reflections on what you observed. What did you learn?

Day 3—Topic 3

_____

Your goal for the topic:

_____

_____

_____

_____

What did you observe about yourself or others?

_____

_____

_____

_____

Capture your reflections on what you observed. What did you learn?

_____

_____

_____

_____

Day 4—Topic 4

_____

Your goal for the topic:

_____

_____

_____

_____

What did you observe about yourself or others?

_____

_____

_____

_____

Capture your reflections on what you observed. What did you learn?

_____

_____

_____

_____

64

Day 5—Topic 5

_____

Your goal for the topic:

_____

_____

_____

_____

What did you observe about yourself or others?

_____

_____

_____

_____

Capture your reflections on what you observed. What did you learn?

_____

_____

_____

_____

Day 6—Topic 6

_____

Your goal for the topic:

_____

_____

_____

_____

What did you observe about yourself or others?

_____

_____

_____

_____

Capture your reflections on what you observed. What did you learn?

_____

_____

_____

_____

Day 7—Topic 7

_____

Your goal for the topic:

_____

_____

_____

_____

What did you observe about yourself or others?

_____

_____

_____

_____

Capture your reflections on what you observed. What did you learn?

_____

_____

_____

_____

Day 8—Topic 8

_____

Your goal for the topic:

_____

_____

_____

_____

What did you observe about yourself or others?

_____

_____

_____

_____

Capture your reflections on what you observed. What did you learn?

_____

_____

_____

_____

Day 9—Topic 9

Your goal for the topic:

What did you observe about yourself or others?

Capture your reflections on what you observed. What did you learn?

Day 10—Topic 10

_____

Your goal for the topic:

_____

_____

_____

_____

What did you observe about yourself or others?

_____

_____

_____

_____

Capture your reflections on what you observed. What did you learn?

_____

_____

_____

_____

Day 11—Topic 11

Your goal for the topic:

What did you observe about yourself or others?

Capture your reflections on what you observed. What did you learn?

Day 12—Topic 12

_____

Your goal for the topic:

_____

_____

_____

_____

What did you observe about yourself or others?

_____

_____

_____

_____

Capture your reflections on what you observed. What did you learn?

_____

_____

_____

_____

Day 13—Topic 13

_____

Your goal for the topic:

_____

_____

_____

_____

What did you observe about yourself or others?

_____

_____

_____

_____

Capture your reflections on what you observed. What did you learn?

_____

_____

_____

_____

Day 14—Topic 14

Your goal for the topic:

What did you observe about yourself or others?

Capture your reflections on what you observed. What did you learn?

Day 15—Topic 15

_____

Your goal for the topic:

_____

_____

_____

_____

What did you observe about yourself or others?

_____

_____

_____

_____

Capture your reflections on what you observed. What did you learn?

_____

_____

_____

_____

Day 16—Topic 16

_____

Your goal for the topic:

_____

_____

_____

_____

What did you observe about yourself or others?

_____

_____

_____

_____

Capture your reflections on what you observed. What did you learn?

_____

_____

_____

_____

Day 17—Topic 17

Your goal for the topic:

What did you observe about yourself or others?

Capture your reflections on what you observed. What did you learn?

Day 18—Topic 18

_____

Your goal for the topic:

_____

_____

_____

_____

What did you observe about yourself or others?

_____

_____

_____

_____

Capture your reflections on what you observed. What did you learn?

_____

_____

_____

_____

Day 19—Topic 19

Your goal for the topic:

What did you observe about yourself or others?

Capture your reflections on what you observed. What did you learn?

Day 20—Topic 20

Your goal for the topic:

What did you observe about yourself or others?

Capture your reflections on what you observed. What did you learn?

Day 21—Topic 21

Your goal for the topic:

What did you observe about yourself or others?

Capture your reflections on what you observed. What did you learn?

Day 22—Topic 22

Your goal for the topic:

What did you observe about yourself or others?

Capture your reflections on what you observed. What did you learn?

Day 23—Topic 23

Your goal for the topic:

What did you observe about yourself or others?

Capture your reflections on what you observed. What did you learn?

Day 24—Topic 24

_____

Your goal for the topic:

_____

_____

_____

_____

What did you observe about yourself or others?

_____

_____

_____

_____

Capture your reflections on what you observed. What did you learn?

_____

_____

_____

_____

Day 25—Topic 25

Your goal for the topic:

What did you observe about yourself or others?

Capture your reflections on what you observed. What did you learn?

Day 26—Topic 26

_____

Your goal for the topic:

_____

_____

_____

_____

What did you observe about yourself or others?

_____

_____

_____

_____

Capture your reflections on what you observed. What did you learn?

_____

_____

_____

_____

Day 27—Topic 27

Your goal for the topic:

What did you observe about yourself or others?

Capture your reflections on what you observed. What did you learn?

Day 28—Topic 28

_____

Your goal for the topic:

_____

_____

_____

_____

What did you observe about yourself or others?

_____

_____

_____

_____

Capture your reflections on what you observed. What did you learn?

_____

_____

_____

_____

Day 29—Topic 29

Your goal for the topic:

What did you observe about yourself or others?

Capture your reflections on what you observed. What did you learn?

Day 30—Topic 30

_____

Your goal for the topic:

_____

_____

_____

_____

What did you observe about yourself or others?

_____

_____

_____

_____

Capture your reflections on what you observed. What did you learn?

_____

_____

_____

_____

Day 31—Topic 31

Your goal for the topic:

What did you observe about yourself or others?

Capture your reflections on what you observed. What did you learn?

CPSIA information can be obtained
at www.ICGtesting.com
Printed in the USA
LVOW08s1757060217
523355LV00002B/544/P